NOW YOU CAN READ ABOUT....
HORSES and PONIES

TEXT BY STEPHEN ATTMORE

ILLUSTRATED BY LIBBY TURNER AND ERIC ROWE

BRIMAX BOOKS • NEWMARKET • ENGLAND

Here is a pony. His name is Ross.
He is a happy pony. Boys
and girls love to ride on Ross.
Look at the long hair on his neck.
This is called his mane. Ross has
a long tail too, but his legs
are short. Can you see the pony's
hooves? These are his feet.

Ross is not a big pony. He is
a Welsh mountain pony. A pony is
a small horse. Ross is four years
old. We can tell the age of
a pony or a horse by its teeth.
Large adult teeth start growing
when the horse or pony is three.

Ross is a father.
Here is his son.
His name is Tiny.

Baby ponies or
baby horses are
called foals.
Tiny is only two
days old. He is
still wobbly on
his feet.

Tiny is being
licked by his
mother. She feeds
him until he is
about six months
old. Tiny will be
a foal until his
first birthday.
Then he will be
a pony.

This girl is measuring Ross. How
tall do you think he is? He is
11 hands tall. One 'hand' is equal
to four inches. Look at the stick
the girl is using. She is measuring
from the ground to the top of his
shoulder. This is how horses
and ponies are measured.

This is the tallest horse in
the world. It is called a Shire
horse. It is very strong.

All ponies are smaller than
14 hands. The Shetland pony is
only nine hands high.

Horses and ponies need love and care. If they are ill you must call a vet. Ross is kept in a stable in winter. His stable is cleaned out each day. New straw is spread over the floor. Ross drinks water and eats hay and bran. He is brushed and taken for a walk every day.

Did you know that horses and ponies wear shoes? They have metal shoes to protect their feet. Look at the blacksmith fitting new shoes. He has cut the horse's hooves. We cut our toenails when they grow too long. Horses and ponies have their hooves cut every six weeks.

Have you ever
watched a horse
moving? Look at
this white horse.
It is walking.
It lifts its feet
in turn. Its tail
is lying down.

Now the horse is
trotting. It is
moving its legs
in pairs. One
front leg and one
back leg are on
the ground at the
same time.

The horse is now going faster. It is running. We call this cantering. Look at its tail. It is swishing about.

The horse is running very fast. We call this galloping. Both of its back legs are off the ground at the same time.

Riding is fun. It is not easy.
You need to learn to ride. Look
at the boy sitting on the pony.
He has learned to sit in the
saddle and hold the reins. His
teacher is leading the pony.

There is a lot
to learn before
a rider can begin
to jump. Look at
this girl riding
Ross. They are
jumping a small
fence.

This big horse is
show-jumping. It
is jumping over
a tall fence.
The rider learned
to ride horses
many years ago.

These horses are racing against each other. The men and women who ride them are called jockeys.

These people are riding horses in a game of polo. They try to hit the ball with their sticks.

Horses are used for work. This is a policeman riding a horse.

Horses are used to round-up cattle and sheep in some countries. They work hard.

Have you ever been to a circus? This is a circus horse.

A long time ago horses pulled coaches. They took people from place to place. Then they began to use motor cars instead. Have you seen horses pulling a coach?

Look at the pony pulling a cart.

Look at these big horses. They
are very strong. Some horses
still work in the fields. The
horses are helping the farmer.

Donkeys, mules and zebras
all belong to the horse family.

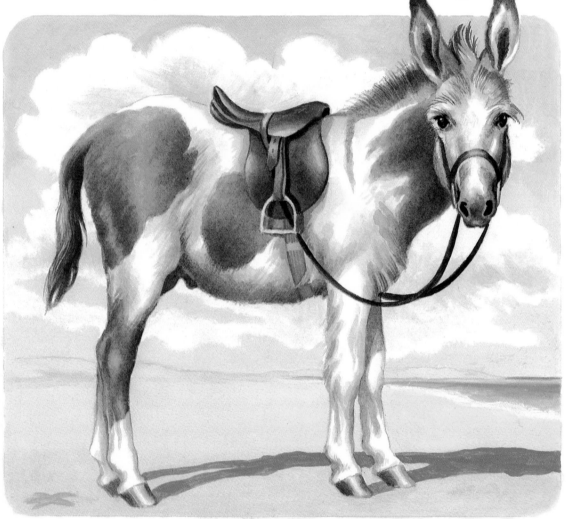

This is a donkey. Look at its big
ears. Have you ever seen donkeys
at the seaside? Boys and girls
ride up and down the beach
on them.

This is a mule.
It looks a bit
like a donkey.
It is bigger and
stronger than
Ross.

A zebra is easy
to spot. It has
black and white
stripes over its
body. It has ears
like a donkey.

In this book you have met Ross. You have seen animals in the horse family. Look for some of them when you go out.

Piebald

Grey

Chestnut

Black

Brown

Markings

Star   Stripe   Snip   Blaze